BUILDING A SUCCESSFUL CAREER WITH ADHD

Connie Naresh

Dedicated to my children with ADHD who are on the launching pad of life.
To guide and inspire you.

Table of Contents

Companion Resources Available

I am happy to provide readers with access to the following tools:

- **Goal Charts** *to aid in planning strategies on how to overcome obstacles,*

- **Identify Your Values Activity Charts,**

- **Side Hustle Ideas** *in your Neighborhood, Community, and Online,*

- **List of Career Choices** *for those who don't like to sit at a desk 9-5,*

 - Net Worth Fill-In Form.

You can have *direct access* to these resources,
which are free to download and print for my subscribers.

YES – I WANT MY FREE SUBSCRIPTION →
http://bit.ly/ConniesResources

2

CHAPTER ONE

Introduction

CHOOSING an occupation we love is important to all of us, but for someone with ADHD, that's a make-or-break question. Most of us stick to a job even if it isn't our dream-come-true occupation. That's not the case with ADHD people. Think of a boring job as Kryptonite for Superman. Every long second ticking toward finishing time drains their life-energy. Those among us with ADHD are hard-wired that way. It seems impossible for people with ADHD to cope with long periods of dreary repetitiveness. Mundane routines can't hold their interest. Astonishingly, the same symptoms that give people with ADHD a bad name are commonly considered top-quality traits in many professional areas. This book helps overcome the stigma of ADHD by explaining how to capitalize on interests and abilities. Join me on a journey to discover how ADHD can be a strength. I like to think of my ADHD friends as folks with unique talents. Just as in everybody else's life, if you play to your talents, you can excel at your job and reach your full potential.

If you or someone in your family has ADHD, you are probably familiar with the concept of productive versus bothersome symptoms. Please understand that you are not alone. ADHD is common around the world. You may struggle in your professional life regardless of your friendly character, helpful attitude, high intelligence and your ability to hyperfocus on an issue while seeing the

4

big picture better than mere mortals. What if you could put an end to colorless workdays for good? What if you could embark on a career path perfectly tailored to your personal gifts?

According to research, 4.4% of the adults in the US struggle with ADHD. I am suggesting the number of undiagnosed cases is even higher. ADHD is common among grown-ups. If you, dear reader, believe that ADHD is holding you back from achieving your potential and fulfilling your aspirations and dreams, hold that thought and read on. There are millions of people who have ADHD and still live successful personal and professional lives. I understand that the symptoms associated with ADHD often lead to personal and professional situations fraught with challenges. Managing life with ADHD can be discouraging and seemingly insurmountable. It does not have to be! I hope to inspire my readers to focus on their potential. Your ADHD strengths can be identified, developed, and used to achieve your professional goals. Your talents are precious, your abilities are unique, and your potential is real.

I will highlight a few of the many people who refused to allow ADHD to hold them back. Instead, they use the amazing spectrum of ADHD dynamics to propel them to succeed. Did you know that Albert Einstein is believed to have had ADHD? Yet, are his theories not regarded some of the most ground-breaking work in the world of physics, even today? Consider Mr. Vincent Van Gogh, one of the greatest impressionist artists of the nineteenth century. He, too, is thought to have struggled with ADHD, but he gifted the world with some of the most beautiful art seen in museums around the globe.

In the world of business, the founder of Virgin Media Group, Richard Branson, also has ADHD. Did he not become the epitome of entrepreneurial success? Does he not own 400 companies around the world?

Have you heard of Katherine Ellison? She is a Pulitzer-prize winning international correspondent and journalist. She broke through the barriers of the news business. Yes, she too, has ADHD.

There is Ed Hallowell, M.D., a Harvard psychiatrist and best-selling author. He did not permit ADHD to hold him back either.

Consider the success stories in film and fashion. One easy to spot culprit is Jim Carrey. We also have Will Smith, Woody Harrelson, Justin Bieber, Ryan Gosling, and Christopher Knight; the list of ADHD greats is endless. No one could have said it better than the actress

Wendy Davis, who is best known for her iconic role in the series Army Wives:

"ADHD makes you different, not defective."

For us neurotypicals, it is paramount to understand that individuals with ADHD have been gifted unique talents. Their abilities may surpass those of other people. As with any potential we purposefully tap into, we direct the brilliance of a person with ADHD in ways that do not limit but support their professional success. Let ADHD not stand in the way of a fulfilling, professional life. Instead, use your unique gift to build a successful career. How?

We identify our strengths and use them to our advantage. We always want to base any important decision on the knowledge of our personality and arm ourselves with a thorough understanding of what makes us tick.

There is one caveat: even though we know that folks with ADHD can excel in their personal and professional lives, they have to prepare diligently and make smarter choices than most. More about this later.

Some traits associated with ADHD have gotten a bad rap because we think of them as counterproductive in certain jobs. Yet, the same characteristics, when applied correctly, will help an individual excel in a different line of work and even outperform their colleagues.

To put it simply–individuals with ADHD can experience a high level of job satisfaction, even exceed expectations if they make analytical choices for their desired profession. A well-thought-out career plan will allow you to turn a handicap into an advantage. It should never be a coin-toss.

Here is an example: individuals with ADHD may find it difficult to pay close attention to details over a sustained period. Let's flip this trait around to your advantage. How many strategic planning roles require us to look at the big picture? I am calling the 30,000 ft planners in corporate executive offices. An elevated-view-talent clears the way for creative and innovative ideas because we are less likely to fixate on smaller details. Many successful CEOs are 30,000 ft type people. Analyzing our strengths and weaknesses is exactly that: casting a critical eye over any symptoms and turning a negative into a positive!

CHAPTER TWO

ADHD in Adults - Myths and Facts

ADHD's notoriety as a disorder helped to create several disadvantageous myths. Unfortunately, this can lead the uninformed to making toxic career choices. Let's look closely at myths versus facts about ADHD in this chapter. As long as you understand the strengths and weaknesses associated with ADHD, are you on the way to making better career choices.

Only when you understand the nuances of this disorder will you equip yourself to play to your strengths. Let's look at common misconceptions about this condition. Gaining understanding will allow people with ADHD to pick their occupation wisely.

MYTH #1: Children Outgrow ADHD as They Enter Adulthood

Fact:

Up to sixty percent of children diagnosed with ADHD continue to be affected into adulthood.

Symptoms may change as a child grows, but ADHD doesn't go away. For instance, hypersensitivity in children with ADHD may turn into chronic restlessness as they mature. Behavioral characteristics may manifest differently in adulthood, but ADHD persists and continues to affect the life of the individual.

Myth #2 People with ADHD Cannot Excel in a Workplace Because of the Lower Intellect Level

Fact:

People with ADHD are usually highly cognitive and may perform certain tasks better than their peers without ADHD. We must understand, ADHD is neither a physical problem nor an intellectual disorder. People with ADHD can perform any job. However, they may experience less-stimulating tasks as tedious and boring. ADHD impairs executive function, but with coaching and practice, executive function can be strengthened.

Myth #3 People with ADHD Find it Difficult to Befriend People or Work in Teams

Fact:

People with ADHD can thrive in small social

settings, particularly one-on-one interactions because of the constant flow of stimulation and above average interpersonal skills. Sometimes large groups can be overstimulating. Many with ADHD connect with other individuals effortlessly but seem to be most productive when interacting with one person at a time or working alone. Working in a small team is no more difficult for them than it is for their peers without ADHD. One word of caution: they often have a very direct approach in voicing their views and their wording may not be tactful. ADHD filters are less inhibitive. In general, social interactions activate creative talents in individuals with ADHD, which in turn stimulates others in the group. There are however cases where additional diagnoses such as Asperger Syndrome can change these dynamics.

MYTH #4 People with ADHD Cannot Function in a Workplace Because of the Side Effects of Medication such as Lethargy or Drowsiness

Fact:

Properly adjusted dosage for treating ADHD symptoms increase a person's focus. It also can help with the negative aspects of impulsivity. ADHD medication does not hinder the job but may improve work performance. Diagnosis of ADHD and proper medication strategies are beyond the scope of this book. Please consult a local, reputable ADHD specialist if you would like to explore how medication may help to address your ADHD symptoms.

MYTH #5 People with ADHD Are Less Productive in the Workplace Because They find it Difficult to Remain Focused for Sustained Periods

Fact:

Yes, people with ADHD may experience difficulty focusing on a specific task. On the opposite end of the spectrum, they may also hyperfocus on an assignment that interests them, which can be an advantage.

CHAPTER THREE
The Ideal Job

CERTAIN jobs lend themselves to ADHD traits better than others. But ADHD characteristics do not necessarily manifest the same way; what may be a wise career choice for one based on their traits, may cause difficulties for others. Every individual will experience ADHD symptoms in different ways. There is no one-size-fits-all job solution for ADHD people.

Do not despair! There is a great way to approach this

problem: Weigh your strong and your delicate sides carefully and measure the scale against the known job requirements. The jobs ticking the most boxes in your strength column are excellent candidates for using your ADHD competitively. I base the job suggestions below on research, personal experience, and years of observations.

I have a growing number of resources on my website advicewithconnie.com that can   assist in setting goals along your career bath. Come over for a visit and check them out.

Job #1 Teacher/Daycare Professional

Do you enjoy engaging with children? Are you interested in impacting young lives positively? Does it excite you when you see others succeed in learning, when they get their feet wet trying something new? If this is you, this could be an ideal job for you!

People with ADHD are often extroverts. They are friendly and their enthusiasm and cheerful attitude is contagious. What better candidate to deal with children? There is no monotony in childcare, None! Ask any mother! The day-to-day activities in a daycare center are exciting enough to keep every child care professional interested day-in day-out. Many typical adults easily wear out trying to keep up with the little ones, but active chil-

dren tend to match the energy level of people with

ADHD.

It is no wonder then: teachers with ADHD are often

the kids' favorites.

Job #2 Artist or Graphic Designer

Do you feel most inspired when you immerse yourself

in drawing or design work, when you play with vibrant

colors or illusive patterns, when you are creating some-

thing new, unique and beautiful? If this is something

you'd enjoy, your creative talent may make you a good

fit for artistic professions.

Creativity is one of the most underrated, yet immensely valuable traits of people with ADHD. They are capable of coming up with awe-inspiring, innovative ideas. These individuals think out of the box, literally. Not all of us regular folks can call ourselves highly creative by any decent standard. But chances are, your new colleague with ADHD over there in the art department puts his creative abilities to use easily. Their passion for creative work almost guarantees their success at such a job.

Job #3 Computer Programmer

ADHD infliction begs for innate order. Consider this one:

1.   Go straight
2.   Drive half a mile
3.   Take a right turn
4.   Drive around one mile
5.   Search for KFC
6.   If 5 = "No Result" and
      time >10 minutes GOTO 3
7.   If KFC found AND if OPEN, Place an order.

A computer programming language is built upon an innate order. A software program is a set of instructions, logically assembled to do a thing. Innovation and creativity are key here, too. Programming may be less colorful than a designer's job, but the excitement of bringing to life something new while solving a complicated puzzle appeals to many ADHD-ers. Here, the hyperfocus trait comes into play.

The abstract nature of digital concepts is something

most ADHD people are grasping with little effort. If you love solving puzzles, if you like pondering complex problems and creating unique solutions, this could be the perfect route for you!

Many of us would dread programming. But if your mind is wired to recognize abstract patterns and derive creative solutions from them, someone else's dread could be your bliss. Writing computer code and debugging endless lines of strings, arrays, declarations and functions is just like solving a gigantic puzzle. The mental stimulation is exponential, and these challenges tend to keep people with ADHD glued to their computer. If this is you, why not try it out? There are many free online programming courses available to test the waters. Programmers are also in high demand and well paid, especially if you focus on niche areas.

Job #4 Actor/Musician

Oh, I have seen it in many of my friends with ADHD. Their thirst for flair and the hunger for the spotlight can be insatiable. Can you sing, dance, and act? If that's you, there is ample opportunity to satisfy your creativity in the entertainment sector.

Many famous actors and musicians have talked about their personal struggle with ADHD. Justin Timberlake, Paris Hilton, and Solange Knowles are only three names of many. They have proven that it is possible to use ADHD to one's advantage, even on the big stage. Adam Levine has also talked publicly about his battle with ADHD in high school and how he managed to work with his doctor to overcome his problems and make the most of his abilities. Any creative art could be a viable career option for a person with ADHD, particularly where the artist is already drawn to music or acting.

JOB #5 Chef

WANTED: More creativity. This time it's the eyes, the nose and the palate. Roasting, baking, charbroiling, grilling, frying, steaming and boiling. Do I have your attention?

Do you enjoy cooking on the weekends? Are you curious about recipes when eating out? Do you care about how food is presented on a plate? Do family and friends love your cooking? Perhaps you have been asked to cater for parties?

If you answered yes, you may already be a gifted chef. If so, why not consider a career in the culinary arts?

If you ever watched any of the cooking contest shows on TV, you have a good idea how much pressure there is upon the chef and the kitchen staff. I have personally cooked hundreds of meals a day, even with ADHD people, and if there is one thing true about a kitchen: It's fast-paced, and it never gets boring. The stimulus for an ADHD-er couldn't be more intense. All of their senses are active. If you love to cook delicious meals under pressure, turning your passion for food into a career may just be *the* recipe for you.

People with ADHD are likely to be hyperfocused on several different tasks in the kitchen. It's a mixed bag: a chef needs to see the big picture but will also have to pay attention to detail. Here is a bonus: this is a highly sociable profession. You are working with kitchen staff, food vendors, and customers daily. No boredom–guaranteed. If cooking under pressure is the thing you're good at, this could be the job reservation you would want to make!

Connie Naresh

Job #6 Fashion Designer/ Stylist

Do you receive compliments for the way you dress? Are you ready to make big, bold fashion statements? Do friends ask you for the latest vogue trend? Do you enjoy dressing stylish? Do you constantly dream up new outfits no one else has thought of? Do you have an eye for fashion trends? Do you obsess about helping your friends to look their best? Look in the mirror–and if the shoe fits, look no further. Fashion designer/ stylist may be the ideal career choice for you!

As someone with ADHD, you are likely to be a visionary person. Put the creative juices flowing through your

30

veins to use and choose a profession in fashion or beauty.

Because people with ADHD are intuitively creative, they can effortlessly come up innovative solutions whatever the challenge; it's a natural process. Jobs in the designer world provide us with a chance to showcase our creativity. It's an in-your-face job, perfect for a person with ADHD.

No boredom here either. Imagine the exciting face of a client who sees their make-over come to life in your studio. A happy customer is a paying customer–and if this is your talent, they will come back!

These lines of work foster our creative talent. It's their

bread and butter. Many corporate jobs are often repetitive, uneventful nine-to-fives. Some workplaces may even discourage creativity, not ideal for ADHD. No concern here for any designer or stylist, the mirror your customer looks into reflects your imagination. The sky is the limit!

Job #7 Advertising Professional

Do you have a keen sense of the next-big-thing? Is looking at the grand-picture your strong point? Are you searching for opportunities to use your creativity to come up with out-of-the-box, smart solutions? If yes, you will feel right at home working for an advertising agency!

The advertising industry is always on the lookout for people who are strong-headed and determined to make their mark in the world. It is yet another profession where an employer values ADHD genius.

Advertising comes in many flavors. They spoil us for choices in this industry. Some picks are: media research analyst, media specialist, target marketing strategist, online advertising coordinator; there are many more. These jobs are demanding and, depending on your choice, could cater to your interests. No dullish days at work. These occupations measure creative performance–and if you persistently create innovative ad campaigns, you'll quickly be at the top of your game.

Job #8 Life Coach

It's great when we succeed in our lives. But how would you feel about helping others to realize their potential? Would it excite you to see someone else achieve his or her goals? Would you feel a sense of accomplishment if you motivated clients and helped them through their struggles? Would it inspire you to work with them and develop a strategy for their professional lives while keeping an eye on the big picture? If that sounds like something that fires you up, why not consider establishing a life coaching business!

A life coach works with clients to help them achieve

their goals. These are in most cases clear deliverables. A client's success becomes your success. What would make this proposition interesting for someone with ADHD? Exceptional life-coaches share a number of qualities. Let's see if you can recognize any of these in your ADHD DNA: strong-headedness, creativity, impulsiveness, consistency, and hyperfocus. Which ones are yours? All five?

Life coaches are determined to prove themselves. They are set in their ways—and they ought to be to succeed. Their high-level of creativity and their impulsiveness serve to inspire the client. Their enthusiasm inspires, excites, draws in, and forces change. And all this comes with a cherry on top: life-coaches are hyperfocused and super-consistent individuals. If you thrive on other people's success that is inspired by your coaching, look no further. I guarantee job satisfaction. Supporting others comes with its own reward. What better way than helping clients to achieve their goals while you fulfill your own dreams?

Job #9 Firefighter/Police/Military

Can you handle the pressure of being in a life-threatening situation? Does the prospect of receiving a daily dose of adrenaline every time you walk in to work excite you? Most importantly, are you compassionate, and do you love helping others? The asks may be big–the sacrifices great, but the satisfaction one experiences on these jobs may well be worth it—to the right person.

Apart from police officers and firefighters, we may also count in the military. Any of these professions present fresh challenges daily. Processes, procedures, and supervising officers provide structure and guidance. Safety first! If adrenaline is your second blood, these occupations may just be right for you. Jobs in the line of duty have a great advantage: Structure. You will receive meticulous training in theory and praxis, something most ADHD people will appreciate. When push comes to shove, initiative, selflessness and creativity save the day while we apply what was taught in training. Working as a team, fellow officers, firefighters and soldiers offer a social cohesion unmatched in other occupations.

Do you recognize your ADHD traits here? Challenge and creativity, yet strict training and structure. Social cohesion, yet self-initiative. A strict set of rules, yet not a day that will be the same. What other jobs give us an opportunity to give back to the community and serve those in need?

Job #10 EMT/ Paramedic/Nurse/Doctor

Do you work well under pressure or are you crushed

by it? Can you make smart, split-second decisions while excitement is rushing through your body? Are you compassionate? Do you have a heart for helping others? If this applies to you, consider one of these careers.

People with ADHD typically thrive on fast-paced jobs. This is one reason they make some of the best paramedics, nurses, and emergency room doctors. If you opt for these professions, your ADHD could be advantageous because you need to make fast, life-saving decisions. These jobs are demanding, their dynamics amazing, pushing the professional to the limit.

An EMT, Emergency Medical Technician is in a class

of its own, rushing to a workplace that changes with every call. EMTs arriving at a scene often find themselves in chaotic situations faced with emergencies that demand super concentration from the individual. Your ADHD hyperfocus talent may help save lives! Personally, I admire EMT personnel. What a sacrifice! What a responsibility! What a labor of love to helping others!

Nurses with years of practice, always anticipating the doctor's next move, knowing what to do before being asked to do it, what dedication, focus and energy required. These are unsung heroes. Are you that hero?

Of course, there are the doctors. Their life may not be

as glamorous as depicted in the famous TV series, *Grey's Anatomy,* but it is just as exciting. Apart from treating their patients, medical professionals must react quickly to sudden changes in a patience condition. Some doctors are super-human diagnosticians. If you want to solve puzzles that have life or death consequences in the real world, that's the job to train for. Doctors must also study a lot, even after becoming an M.D. because medical science advances as fast as technology does. If you are a life-long learner and fully dedicated to the medical profession, this could be for you.

JOB #11 Tech-Inventor

Not the M.D. for the body, but the doctor for all-things

tech! We are surrounded by technology. It's ever changing and challenging us regular folks to adapt constantly. It is exciting for those of us who love to look under the hood and figure out how things work and make them work better. Whether it's the nitty gritty of a complex server update, the latest phone models, new cars, or the internet of things that integrates everyday items and connects them via the web. There are as many jobs in tech as there are fish in the sea. We already explored the computer programmer route as a specific field in technology. Here, the choices are even greater. Anything that has a button and a light requires maintenance and development.

Consider the invention of quantum computing–it has become reality. And hidden in plain sight, new life saving concepts in planes, trains, and cars are developed every day. It's an adventure with infinite potential for the techies among us. Creativity here is a must-have. If you are a tech-inventor, what better way to earn a living than developing new technology or inventing groundbreaking methods that make life easier for scientists, producers and end users?

JOB #12 Private Investigator/ Detective

Puzzles. Different ones this time. Are you good at solving mysteries and connecting the dots? Have you figured out the plot of a thriller before the rest of the family

Connie Naresh

has? Can you guess the outcome of a book even before turning the page to the last chapter? If so, you may harbor talents perfect for a PI or a detective.

PI and detective jobs require administrative work. If this is not you, don't despair. Partner up with someone and combine forces. These jobs can excite in their own right as they challenge you to think of new and innovative ways to uncover secrets and outsmart the subject of your investigation. Collecting evidence, carrying out surveillance, performing background checks, uncovering clues, and finding the missing pieces of a puzzle will keep you engaged 24/7.

If you are like most people with ADHD, you already know how easy it is for you to see the bigger picture. What seems to be a perplexing mystery to the average person, you can easily decode. PI work provides a great number of specialization potential. Whatever your particular field of interest, there are plentiful opportunities for investigative work. No match for ADHD people.

JOB #13: Television Producer

Now, this is a profession where creativity has a knock-on effect. For example, (1) you have an idea, and (2) you oversee its production. Just imagine a job where you are paid to come up with interesting ideas for movies or TV shows, pitch them to television networks and also play a managing role in their production. That's the job of a television producer!

Being a television producer is fun, but it's also hectic and chaotic. This role requires physical stamina and great mental capability. The responsibilities are too many to mention here; suffice to say, a TV producer is in charge of every aspect of a production. Add acting and action and we may have a full drama on our hands that requires quick thinking and a decisive person to control. The added bonus? Working with amazing artists and some of the most talented people in the business.

This is a job where the work location changes regularly. Only apply if you enjoy traveling.

Job #14: Journalist

Have you ever thought of a journalist as an adventurist? Yes, journalists are investigators, too. They gather, assess, report and present information. A journalist loves writing, reading, and most of all, truth.

The job of a journalist is difficult. It comes with challenges and moral responsibilities. Not everyone is built for this work. However, people with ADHD can be perfect for this type of employment. Their ability to hyperfocus on an issue, to pursue a matter, and to go out of their way and uncover the facts makes them ideal candidates for journalism. Getting access to information often requires that very ingenuity and level of determination that I have personally seen in people with ADHD. As with PI and detective work, the field of specialization is wide. Anything newsworthy goes.

This reminds me of a prolific journalist: Clarence Page. Mr. Page has ADHD. It runs in the family; his son also has ADHD. This didn't prevent Clarence from winning the Pulitzer Price. Twice. The first time in 1972 for the Chicago Tribune on voter fraud, and again in 1989, this time for his commentaries. Sandwiched in between are three other venerated awards. Mr. Page wrote three books: What Killed Leanita McClain? Showing My Color:

Impolite Essays on Race and Identity, and A Foot in Each

World: Essays and Articles by Leanita McClain, Clarence

Page.

His articles are syndicated in 170 papers. He regularly

appears on National TV. To top it, he is an actor (Rising

Sun).

To sum up how Mr. Page can be so successful despite

his ADHD:

*"Clarence says journalism was a 'perfect' match for him.
The writing is short, he says, there's always a deadline. That
makes it a lot easier to stay on track."*

I rest my case.

Job #15: Sports Athlete

The world of sports offers many career possibilities. Statistics speak against anyone excelling at sports and making it to pro level, earning millions of dollars in this career field. However, some do make it that far.

We know of countless renowned athletes who struggled with ADHD, yet winning gold medals or Super Bowl rings. For instance, Justin Gatlin, Olympic champion in the 100 meters sprint, was diagnosed with

ADHD. He once answered a reporter who asked him about his struggles with ADHD:

"Nothing could stop me — not even ADD."

Chris Kaman, who was selected sixth overall in the first round of the 2003 NBA draft by the Los Angeles Clippers also talked about ADHD. In his own words,

"If I mess up, I mess up. I don't let ADD (ADHD) bring me down."

Michael Phelps, Cammi Granato, Terry Bradshaw, and Pete Rose are some of the many star athletes with ADHD. People with ADHD are often perfectly knit to excel in careers related to sports. Research suggests that

51

children and teenagers with ADHD are often more natu-

rally attracted to sports and enjoy it tremendously. There

is a reason for it: athletic activities increase the number of

neurotransmitters in the brain. The increase helps to re-

lieve many of the unwanted side-effects of ADHD over a

prolonged period. Even if you're not a professional ath-

lete and have no desire to become one, daily physical ex-

ercise can help to cope with ADHD easier.

Doug Hyun Han, MD, PhD, of Chung Ang University

Hospital in South Korea and his colleagues carried out a

series of experiments to explore the relationship between

ADHD and success in the world of sports. His research

suggests that *"ADHD may be more common in elite athletes*

than in the general population, since children with ADHD may be drawn to sports due to the positive reinforcing and attentional activating effects of physical activity. Common symptoms of ADHD may enhance athletic performance. Some athletes with ADHD naturally excel in baseball and basketball, which involve quick movements and reactive decision-making, due to these athletes' inherent impulsivity."

The bottom line is this: Regular sports activities are likely to have a therapeutic effect on individuals with ADHD. Let's not discount the fact that physical activities provide a healthy way to release all the pent-up energy. Accomplishments increase confidence, moral, and overall quality of life.

A full-time career in sports is out of reach for most people. However, the percentage of athletes with ADHD is high, showing that those with ADHD may have a slight edge over those without. Even if you're not into the performance sports yourself, becoming a hard-hitting sports coach could be another career choice worth exploring. (See also Job #8: Life Coach.)

1.	Chef	• Oversee the food preparation at a restaurant or other dining establishment • Typical minimal requirement is a high school diploma • Median salary: $40,630
2.	Police / Correctional Officer	• Responsible for public safety or overseeing individuals who have been arrested, awaiting trial or those who are serving jail time • Typical requirement is a high school diploma • Median salary: $39,020
3.	Firefighter	• Typically only requires a high school diploma or equivalent • Prior emergency / medical services training can be beneficial • An on-the-job training program is mandatory to test physical endurance • Average salary: $49,080
4.	Nurse	• Provide care under the direction of registered nurses and doctors and monitor patients' health and maintain patient records • Typically requires a postsecondary nondegree award • Median salary: $40,380
5.	Postal Service Worker	• Collect, sort, process, and distribute mail • Requires a high school diploma or equivalent and an excellent driving record is necessary • Average salary: $57,260

Figure 1 Careers

Additional Career Ideas and relevant market research

charts can be download from advicewithconnie.com or

viewed in Chapter Eight.

CHAPTER FOUR

Doing Your Own Thing

WE have established that there are countless career options for those challenged with ADHD. I could have listed many more salaried occupations suitable for ADHD people. But that's not the only way of thinking. There may be an even better option to earn a living.

Operating your own business is not for the faint of heart, but it is a career option someone with ADHD should consider. It's backed up by research, too: "...*individuals with ADHD are almost two times more likely to venture into new business ideas. Entrepreneurial action may be a constructive outlet regardless of whether a venture is ultimately founded and successful.*"

Success in business takes fierce determination, consistent execution, and risk-taking. Some of the traits associated with ADHD often characterize the successful business owner because these qualities are indeed needed in order succeed as an entrepreneur. If applied constructively, they can support a business owner's resolve to take the necessary leaps through perseverance when the going gets tough.

Attention, Problem Solvers: if you are someone who people look to as a go-to person because you are constantly seeking to improve a situation, you could turn that ability into a legitimate business. The drive to creating solutions, having an appetite to take calculated risks, an eagerness to move forward, and a determination to persevere are the foundations on which entrepreneurial success is built. They're undaunted by the fire that drives them to keep moving forward. They execute.

How To Measure Success The Right Way

Success does not look the same to everyone, this is obvious. This book is meant to inspire and encourage you in your pursuit of a right-fit career path. How to run a multi-billion-dollar public corporation is beyond the scope of this book nor is it the measure of success I want to elevate as its standard.

Money is not the only determining factor when measuring success either. Earning money is important, for sure. However, if financial gain is all that matters, the reward will be hollow. Our pursuit of success from our career or entrepreneurial choice needs to match our values. When our professional life reflects our innermost values, we are more likely to experience satisfaction. That's the currency we should bank on.

I provided a free Value Evaluation chart in the resource chapter. It is also available for download via advicewithconnie.com. Why not use this tool to find out what matters to you and determine what your personal values are? Going through these steps is a simple exercise. This process helps you identify what is truly important to you, which will bring you one step closer to considering the elements that need to be in some way linked to a fulfilling career. If operating your own business is the path you choose, then the most rewarding type of business will be one that reflect your values closely.

Types of Entrepreneurial Ventures

WE can describe entrepreneurship as launching and running a new business venture. However, there are different types of entrepreneurial paths you could consider.

SMALL Business Entrepreneurship

Small business entrepreneurship refers to a company that operates with the primary goal of making a living to support yourself and your family. While the venture may be profitable, its aim is to fulfill personal needs.

Small business entrepreneurship is most alluring for people with ADHD because it allows them to put their creativity and impulsiveness to work. From management to administrative responsibilities, this venture offers a variety of business tasks, keeping things interesting. The low-to-mid risk and the personal nature of a small business make this option a sure fit for some with ADHD.

Small business ventures include businesses like a hairdresser's shop, a rental company, a grocery store, a bakery or coffee shop, and trade businesses such as plumbers and electricians, consultants, and freelancers.

SCALABLE Startup Entrepreneurship

Do you think your business could change your life and also add high value to society? If so, let's consider a scalable startup entrepreneurship. The funding for this venture comes from investors. Most people embark on these enterprises with a business partner. You may start the business on your own but eventually will hire employees. The aim is to generate funds for product and service development, their marketing and launch. The draw-back is the accountability to investors. Decisions may not be solely our own anymore, because we're working with other-people's money.

This approach requires patience. It can be a long-term

struggle, and it may take dozens of months before your business reaches its full potential. But as the persistent ADHD person you are, you see the big picture. With patience, determination, and an ever-flowing river of innovative ideas, the years of hard work may pay-off and provide your family with income for generations to come. If you are ready to dive into the venture of a life-time and have a solution that benefits a large group of the population, then definitely consider a startup venture.

Along the way, difficulties will present themselves, obstacles must be overcome. From a young age, the ADHD person knows what it means to be confronted by struggles above and beyond the norm. School–the challenge to focus–has taught grit. ADHD-ers understand the importance of charging ahead and making the most of every situation. Those gritty qualities produce an ability to push through when the going gets tough. It's that combination along with a great idea that is vital to building a successful business. Hardships and struggles have a way of miraculously molding us into individuals who know how to face adversity without suffering defeat.

Whichever enterprise someone chooses, perseverance, problem solving and grit are required. If you think your path of ADHD has deposited these qualities into your life, then it would be smart to explore starting your own entrepreneurial venture.

CHAPTER FIVE

Consider a Side Hustle

MAYBE you are on a decent career path but crave stimulation. Perhaps you need a few hundred dollars extra a month to go on vacation or pay the bills. Consider a side hustle. Losing interest and getting bored with routine is a common problem for people with ADHD. Boredom is Kryptonite. You always want to look for an exciting career that will hold your interest. However, it may be difficult to land a dream job or to start a business. There is a third way to make your life more interesting, even generate a profit. Let's look for a side hustle. Making additional money with a hobby is a great way to keep life exciting and add to your monthly cash flow.

A side hustle can be any income generating opportunity that may be started quickly with little risk. This is not a full-time career. A side hustle is intended to add another stream of income that puts extra cash in your pocket and is often birthed from a hobby. For instance, you might love photography and you're good at it. It is something you already do. Why not put your creative talent and hobby equipment to good use? You could turn your recreational activity into a side business. You could offer your service to event planners or sell your pictures online. In today's age of online media, unique and creative photos can be a viable source of income

The world of social media offers another opportunity that could help you to turn your passion into a side business. If you love engaging with others online, if you are a maverick, becoming a social media manager may bring in some extra cash. I regularly see Wanted ads for Social Media Influencers on freelancing platforms.

How about travel? I have seen video blogs with hundreds of thousands of followers. Whatever your interests, there is no reason not to use your talents to consider a side hustle. It's a great option for people with ADHD. Even if money may not be your first objective, such venture keeps the ADHD person focused and filled with purpose. Who knows, a small side hustle may turn into a full-time, scalable gig.

Freelancing is another good option for people with ADHD for the same reasons: you can start small, try before you buy, enjoy what you do, add value to others, and increase your cash flow. Just scan some freelance job boards online and see what skills are in demand. Thinking further: if there is a particular job in high demand that matches your interests, you could train for it.

Freelancing as a side hustle smells of ultimate freedom. Earn additional money at your convenience. Keep in mind though, freelancers work in the real world with real clients who have deadlines, high expectations and a lot to lose if we mess up. It doesn't get boring.

Low-Risk Side Hustle Ideas

HERE are even more low-risk side hustle ideas.

Dog walking

Do you love animals? Why not walk dogs in the neighborhood? What better way than spending time with dogs of all colors and breeds and getting paid for it? Apart from the financial bonus, dog walking also adds regular exercise to our daily routine. It is perfect for an ADHD person, because dog walking is a stress-busting activity that will keep the serotonin level high and boost your mood. Research shows that people who spend time with pets, especially dogs, are more content with their lives. Therefore, this side hustle works well for people with ADHD. It will not only give you a healthy outlet for all that pent-up energy and improve your mood, it will also help you earn a little extra cash–truly a win-win situation!

Babysitting

Looking after a child, even for a few hours, is not an easy job. It requires our full attention and we can't turn our back on the little ones, not even for a second. However, what's one person's difficulty may be an ADHD person's bliss, because they can hyperfocus while caring for the children. Kids are little bundles of joy and energy and are likely to keep your hands full. Did you know, children closely match an ADHD person's energy level, while most non-ADHD people tire quickly given children's constant need for attention? As an ADHD person, that's not your problem.

Coaching

I mentioned Life Coach as a profession earlier in the book (see Job #8: Life Coach). The option here is similar but different. A coach is an expert in a particular field who helps people to improve their performance. If you are good at something, don't let your talent go to waste. Why not consider becoming a part-time coach? Use your skills to add value to someone else's life and earn a little extra on the side. Teach what you are good at. Are you great at a particular sport? Could you show children or adults the tricks of the trade? Parents, even schools often look for coaches to interest their children in sports.

I can also think of a swimming coach, gym trainer, business consultant, guitar teacher–the choices are endless. Online opportunities give us even more options. Perhaps you speak more than one language? Online language tutors are always wanted. Take your pick - as long as you are good at it. Remember, we want to add value in everything we do.

Tech Helper

While it may not be true for everyone, most baby boomers, Gen-X, and even some millennials are not as tech-savvy as younger people. Technology is evolving at super-sonic speed, and it is difficult to keep up with it all the time. If you are into tech, it works in your favor. You could offer tech support to folks in your neighborhood, even around the town or city. Generally, it doesn't take more than a single visit to solve a tech-related problem. Sometimes, fixing issues remotely may do the trick.

If you love technology as much as I love chocolate, this side hustle may be the perfect venue to putting your tech skills to good use and earn a little extra in your free time. Start with family and friends. Soon, word goes out, and that's worth gold. It won't hurt to advertise a bit, and soon calls for tech support will come in frequently. It is exciting to help people. Each solved issue and every happy client serve to increase our sense of self-worth and quality of life. Such an enterprise requires only little investment on our part: just a computer, knowledge, good manners and a genuine desire to help others. Puzzle solvers to the rescue!

Crafts on Etsy

What's Etsy.com? I love it! It's a hub for selling home-made goodies. Anything we can imagine, from customized notebooks and hand-made mobile phone covers to unique shirts and shoes. It is a platform for small home businesses that offers immense potential for growth. If your product is in demand, look at expanding your home crafts shop soon. Organic business growth!

We already know, folks with ADHD are naturally creative and are on the look-out to try something new and exciting. Once they found something that holds their interest, they usually see the project through to the end. ADHD qualities lend themselves to creative ventures such as offering crafts on Etsy. Let your creativity run wild. If your product takes off, so will the customer base, perhaps not only on Etsy, but on the many other craft-platforms out there, such as ArtFire, Amazon Handmade, eCRATER, Big Cartel, and Zibbet. Why not create your own crafts store on two or more of these sites? It's a great way to learn the ropes of small business through advertising, communication via customer interaction, shipping, and accounting. Arts & Business – Could this be your dream business combination?

Social Media Manager

I alluded to this option in my opening to our side hustles. Social media are big business. They are also time-consuming, and not all business owners are socialites with enough time on their hands to enthuse potential customers and create an online presence that makes a difference to the business and its customers. This job is in high-demand. I can see ADHD mavericks getting a kick out of managing the social media accounts for a business. It is a field that requires focus and an authoritative, yet friendly presence. If you are a social media enthusiast, and if you already spend a lot of time on places like Facebook, Twitter or Instagram, this could be a perfect side hustle for you. Managing multiple social media accounts requires coordination skills, focus and dedication. This job can be a handful–but so can be the cash that rolls in. Social Media influencers for business are artists, too. I won't bore you with terms such as 'Search Engine Optimization' but fact is, you could use your enthusiasm for social media to help a business succeed. It beats chatting for hours-on-end without getting payed. You will interact with many interesting people online. Much of the physical market place is transitioning into the virtual world. The hustle and bustle of the social media universe and the responsibility of representing a company online has its own appeal, perhaps especially to an ADHD brain.

Did I mention creative abilities? You've got them–and they're useful here, too. Representing a business and drawing in potential customers starts with creating engaging content that attracts new followers. Online marketing is highly lucrative. Most businesses prefer to outsource management of their social media accounts as they rarely have the in-house knowledge and resources to manage their online world. It's a fantastic opportunity for those social account pros with ADHD. If you are knowledgeable about online marketing, and if you enjoy

the busy dynamics of social media, look into this oppor-

tunity. Clients always advertise on freelancing platforms

like Fiver and Guru. You could also check with local

businesses and add personal flair to your relationship

with them and customize your approach to online mar-

keting. Let's go–Maverick! Become a trend setter for a

business!

Tutoring

Most students with ADHD have had a hard time pay-

ing attention. School grades were in most cases unkind

and unreflective of ones' true abilities. It may come as a

surprise then that this doesn't mean that people with

ADHD are not good at studying or even teaching. As long as the subject engages the students' mind, they're likely to outperform their classmates. Do you remember a subject you were fond of in school? Perhaps you've become an expert in a certain field? This could be your groundwork laid for offering private tutoring locally or online.

Knowing the pitfalls of learning in groups with people without ADHD qualifies the person with ADHD to be an excellent tutor. It's not about good grades with tutoring. It's about learning, information retention and training.

You can also opt for online tutoring. Many learners turn to the internet to look for solutions to their tutoring needs. An opportunity with an international clientele potential. Whether you are teaching art related skills, math, or languages, online tutoring could be the perfect side hustle for anyone with a webcam, a good microphone and a reliable internet connection.

All these options are just that – ideas. Have you already come up with dozens more? Everything honest and ethical goes. The only thing that is holding you back is your unbelief. Your God-given talents are precious and valuable. Granted, there are serious challenges that ADHD presents, but there are also valuable strengths that can be used for good. Let's turn the stigma of ADHD around by focusing on the strengths you do possess. These qualities can add value to your own career choices and positively impact the lives of those around you.

A side hustle may be the perfect creative outlet for your ADHD strengths to shine with minimal risk. If you are still unconvinced, consider the story in the following chapter. It's an inspiring real-life account of a young student with ADHD who has proven that ADHD is not an excuse–it's an opportunity!

For additional Side Hustle ideas visit

advicewithconnie.com or goto Chapter Eight.

CHAPTER SIX

An Inspirational Story

Allan Maman–The Teenage Entrepreneur

THE fidget spinner craze took the world by storm. It is famous among children and teenagers. It even gained a reputation for being a stress-buster. When Allan Maman first heard about the fidget spinner, he instantly knew he wanted one. However, the trend was relatively new and had not hit the market yet. Allan couldn't get one without waiting several weeks for delivery. Since waiting isn't something he's fond of, he made his own fidget spinner.

With the help of his teacher, he used the 3D printer in the high school science lab in Armonk, NY to print his very own fidget spinner. As he had expected, his self-made device sparked great interest among his fellow students. Everyone wanted to own one!

Allan saw the bigger picture and realized the potential of fidget spinners. He began to spend his evenings in the lab, printing hundreds of fidget spinners that he then sold to his classmates. In just a few weeks, he made two hundred dollars. Soon the school administrators took no-

tice and barred him from continuing his little venture.

Luckily, Allan had earned enough money to buy his

own 3D printer. Partnering up with his student buddy

Cooper Weis, he launched an online store only for fidget

spinners. They called it Fidget360. His timing was per-

fect–the fidget spinner craze was just kicking off. Accord-

ing to a report by Forbes, since the fall of 2016, Allan and

Cooper shipped 3D fidget spinners to all 50 states and to

thirty countries, ringing up over $350,000 in profits.

Making use of his ADHD strengths, Allan and his

friend went beyond the conventional spinners available

in the marketplace. They took their own creative take on fidget spinners and came up with appealing designs and innovative models. For instance, they called one of their spinners Batman: it looked like a small bat that the user could rotate. Such original ideas helped to grow their consumer base rapidly. They also put time and effort into social media marketing to boost their business. They ended up gaining over 160,000 followers on Instagram.

The demand for their fidget spinners was so great that Allan and Cooper started printing from a factory in Brooklyn. They hired many of their friends and even donated a brand-new 3D printer to the school lab as a way of giving back.

For Allan, this successful venture was more than just making money with the latest gimmick. As someone who knew and understood the quirks of ADHD, Allan took this opportunity to help other children who experienced similar problems with their attention deficit.

In an interview with Mic, Allan said, *"I recognized them as a phenomenon the first week I started selling them at school. Literally every kid came up to me, asking me to get one."*

However, it wasn't easy for Allan. In the interview he

said: *"I would say that initially a lot of adults probably saw fidget spinners and thought they were a dumb idea. When I first started and showed my parents what I was making, they were like, 'OK, so it spins. There's nothing special or too neat about it.' But once you see how good it is to have it in class and how fun it is and how everyone wants one, you get it."*

Can you see it? Allan used his unique abilities to project the bigger picture. He developed his idea, paying no attention to what others thought. Talking about his plans for the future, Allan said, *"I definitely don't think the fidget spinner will last into the new school year in September."* Therefore, he and Cooper diversified their products. Allan believes that he can identify the trends in the market, which help him grow his business. ADHD forward thinking!

"I have people all over, looking for the next fidget spinner," Allan said. *"I have distributors in China I talk to now. Whenever they get a big order for a new product or develop something new and fun, they let me know,"* revealed Allan.

This ADHD teenager followed his passion for fidget spinners all the way to owning and operating a successful toy business. Despite the troubles he faced along the path, Allan was hyperfocused on his venture, driving it to success. His ADHD abilities allowed him to turn a simple idea into a profitable enterprise. He transformed his ADHD quirks into strength, and this is the core message of this book. Your ADHD traits are not disabilities but opportunities with unlimited potential.

Allan did all this while at high school. Energy, vision, creativity, and the will to turn an idea into a business may just be the get-out-of-jail-card some people with ADHD need in order to focus their creative energies in a positive direction, no matter their age.

CHAPTER SEVEN

Conclusion

BUILDING a Successful Career with ADHD

People with ADHD may be cut out for many jobs. We recognize ADHD strengths are powerful, potential catalysts to become very successful in a short amount of time. But let us not underestimate the drawbacks of ADHD that could be counterproductive to success.

Any ADHD related career decision has to result from a careful analysis of your strengths and weaknesses. Here are a few things that can help you on your way!

Reflect

One of the best and most useful qualities of people with ADHD is that they can make split-second decisions with little hesitation. The negative connotation is: You are impulsive. Decisiveness works well in some jobs and is frowned upon in others. Reflect on what the requirements of any job are and compare them carefully to your own traits. Awareness of your weaknesses is strategic because you can find people to fill in the gaps you may lack so that the tasks or things you hate won't turn into career roadblocks.

You know yourself well. However, I have found it useful to gather 360-feedback–asking people around me how they see me. This process is part of an honest, self-critical analysis designed to improve performance. Start with people you trust and who know you well. Family members, your kids, friends, perhaps a neighbor or sports team buddy.

Have you ever looked at a photograph and not recognized yourself right away? What? This is me? No way... Or did you love to sing your heart out in the shower knowing you sounded amazing until someone played a recording of your singing back to you? Oh, the shock.

THAT's NOT MY VOICE! I have been there. Blushingly!

To avoid such embarrassment in real life, particularly as

an ADHD person, the 360-feedback can show us a mirror

with a reflection we don't always expect. What we may

perceive as weakness could be seen by others as a virtue–

and vice versa.

We always want to analyze carefully the requirements

of a potential job. When you are interviewed, ask ques-

tions. Employers love candidates who are inquisitive.

Applicants with genuine interest usually make it to the

top of the shortlist. If your questions reveal aspects of the

job that you may find difficult to cope with, you could

discuss options with the hiring manager and HR to see if

they can adapt this job to suit your strengths. If that's not the case and you decide this role isn't for you, that's a win, too.

PICK **What You Enjoy**

When choosing a career path, we weigh factors such as remuneration, working hours, or location. The most important factor for any ADHD person, however, must be your interests and inclinations. No matter how well paid, how alluring the corporate title, or how convenient the working hours may be, if you are not genuinely interested in that field of work, stay clear of signing the dotted line.

Most people without ADHD take up their cross and endure a job they are not interested in. ADHD people generally cannot cope. The Kryptonite becomes even stronger poison. As a person with ADHD, you can safely eliminate half of the potential downfalls associated with ADHD in the workplace with careful analysis of yourself and the role. There are no sure bets – but you can prepare and align your strengths and interests with the requirements of a job.

SEEK Help and Get Guidance

The sun doesn't always shine in ADHD land. To avoid hardships and build a successful career, you need to learn to deal with the negative aspects of ADHD. Medication can reduce or eliminate symptoms. Others develop personal coping mechanisms or use physical exercise to mitigate negative effects of ADHD. Awareness of negative traits is key (see the 360-feedback technique in the previous section.) It is okay to humble ourselves and seek guidance whenever we need it. Your willingness to improve yourself will help you to flourish in the long run; and that's a perfect recipe for reaching your full potential at work.

FINALLY, Don't Settle for Less

You are made wonderfully with ADHD, or without it. You are a miracle. Don't settle for less just because

ADHD affects you. It may take time to reach your full potential, to find your ideal occupation, or to create the perfect side hustle, but keep growing! Don't give up when you are discouraged. Never throw-in the towel when disappointment visits. Move forward instead. I hope this book will help you to build a career based on your ADHD strengths. Go ahead, discover your true potential, realize your personal aspirations and experience a fulfilling personal and professional life.

For more resources and reference material from Connie please subscribe to her web-site via

www.advicewithconnie.com.

CHAPTER EIGHT

Resources

1.	Chef	• Oversee the food preparation at a restaurant or other dining establishment • Typical minimal requirement is a high school diploma • Median salary: $40,630
2.	Police / Correctional Officer	• Responsible for public safety or overseeing individuals who have been arrested, awaiting trial or those who are serving jail time • Typical requirement is a high school diploma • Median salary: $39,020
3.	Firefighter	• Typically only requires a high school diploma or equivalent • Prior emergency / medical services training can be beneficial • An on-the-job training program is mandatory to test physical endurance • Average salary: $49,080
4.	Nurse	• Provide care under the direction of registered nurses and doctors and monitor patients' health and maintain patient records • Typically requires a postsecondary nondegree award • Median salary: $40,380
5.	Postal Service Worker	• Collect, sort, process, and distribute mail • Requires a high school diploma or equivalent and an excellent driving record is necessary • Average salary: $57,260

Figure 1 Careers

6.	Construction Foreman	• Foreman overseeing a construction project or equipment operators maneuvering heavy machinery used in the construction of roads, bridges, buildings, etc. • Typical requirement is a high school diploma • Median salary: $39,460
7.	Athletic Trainer	• Specializes in diagnosing and treating muscle and bone injuries • Typically requires a Bachelor's degree • Median salary: $41,600
8.	Carpenter	• Construct and repair building frameworks and structures • Typically requires a high school diploma • Attending a trade school may be beneficial • Average salary: $51,150
9.	Real Estate Broker	• Typically requires a minimum of a high school diploma and additional coursework to obtain certification • Average salary: $56,730
10.	Landscaper	• A minimum of a Bachelor's degree may be preferred, especially in Landscape Architecture • Average salary: $65,760
11.	Funeral Director	• Educational requirements are minimal with most requiring a high school diploma • Licensure is required before obtaining a director position, for which training can be received on the job • Average salary: $56,850

Figure 2 Careers

12.	Railroad Jobs	• A variety of positions are available from engineers to conductors and management positions • These roles typically only require a high school diploma or equivalent and on-the-job training • Average salary: $59,780
13.	Criminal Investigator	• Interview individuals and collect evidence in support of specific cases • These jobs require a high school diploma or equivalent and prior experience in law enforcement is preferred • There is also on-the-job training expected • Average salary: $58,582
14.	Electrician	• Installing and maintaining electrical systems in homes, factories and office buildings • Requires apprenticeship / technical training program • Median salary: $55,190
15.	Restaurant Manager	• Handling all management, administrative and customer service tasks that help a restaurant run smoothly • Annual salary range: $31,580 to $92,410 or more • Projected job growth: 9 percent

Figure 3 Careers

16.	Mechanic	• Fix and service automobiles on a regular basis, working with your hands and technological tools • Annual salary range: $23,420 to $66,950 or more • Projected job growth: 6 percent	
17.	Teacher	• Share knowledge of a wide range of subjects and ignite the imaginations of children • Annual salary range: $35,680 to $97,500 or more • Projected job growth: 7 percent	
18.	EMT / Paramedic	• Respond to emergency calls for medical help and help save lives • Annual salary range: $22,760 to $58,640 or more • Projected job growth: 15 percent	
19.	Salesperson	• Selling a company's products and services and earn income as a percentage of sales • Ability to work independently and set your own pace • Annual salary range: $26,300 to $116,090 or more • Projected job growth: 5 percent	
20.	Truck Driver	• Delivering items with clear directives from point A to point B • Spend independent time cruising on the road; loading, unloading and preparing truck requires physical stamina • Annual salary range: $28,160 to $65,260 or more • Projected job growth: 6 percent	

Top 3 Measurable Goals to Accomplish in the Next 3 Months	Target Dates	Perceived Obstacles & Potential Solutions	Weekly Progress Toward Goals
Goal 1	Goal 1 Date	Obstacle	1 2
Action Steps 1	1	Solutions	3 4 5
2	2	Obstacle	6 7 8
3	3	Solutions	9 10
Reward			11 12
Goal 2	Goal 2 Date	Obstacle	1 2
Action Steps 1	1	Solutions	3 4 5
2	2	Obstacle	6 7 8
3	3	Solutions	9 10
Reward			11 12
Goal 3	Goal 3 Date	Obstacle	1 2
Action Steps 1	1	Solutions	3 4 5
2	2	Obstacle	6 7 8
3	3	Solutions	9 10
Reward			11 12

Figure 4 Careers

Figure 5 Goal Action Plan

Building a Successful Career with ADHD

Circle What You Value

Faith Trust Peace Hope Gratitude Work Honesty Discipline Courage
Integrity Forgiveness Respect Community Character Decency Kindness
Sense Equality Fairness Standards Honor Authenticity Collaboration
People Innovation Happiness Courage Commitment Passion Focus
Openness Strength Tenacity Efficiency Helpfulness Logic Understanding
Skill Modesty Flexibility Curiosity Enthusiasm Decisiveness Warmth
Ambition Achievement Humility Timeliness Generosity Fun Organization
Persistence Love Intelligence Diligence Sacrifice Loyalty Mindfulness
Freedom Dedication Clarity Adaptability Drive Intuitiveness Speed

Figure 6 Identifying Values Step 1

Choose 12 Values That Matter Most to You

1 _____   5 _____   9 _____
2 _____   6 _____   10 _____
3 _____   7 _____   11 _____
4 _____   8 _____   12 _____

Figure 7 Identifying Values Step 2

Narrow Down Your Top 6 Values

1 _____   3 _____   5 _____
2 _____   4 _____   6 _____

Figure 8 Identifying Values Step 3

Top 3 Values

3 _____

2 _____

1 _____

The Most Important Value to You

Figure 9 Identifying Values Step 4

NET WORTH CALCULATOR

DATE [   ]

ASSETS		LIABILITIES	
Checking Accounts	$	Accounts Payable	$
Savings Accounts	$	Credit Card Debt	$
Other Cash Accounts	$	Unpaid Taxes	$
Investments	$	Student Loans	$
401(k) / IRAs	$	Vehicle Loans	$
Pension / Social Security	$	Mortgage	$
Other Retirement Accounts	$	Home Equity Loans	$
Vehicles	$	Other Liabilities	$
Market Value of Residence	$		
Other Property	$		
Other Assets	$		
TOTAL ASSETS	**$**	**TOTAL LIABILITIES**	**$**
NET WORTH (Total Assets - Total Liabilities)			**$**

Compliments of Connie Naresh
www.advicewithconnie.com

Figure 10 Net Worth Calculator

Side Hustles
In Your Neighborhood

1. Baby sitting
2. Senior care
3. Yard and lawn care
4. Dog walking
5. Dog sitting
6. Party catering
7. Tutoring
8. Pool cleaning
9. Tree trimming
10. Garbage removal
11. Junk hauling
12. Clothing alterations
13. Car washing
14. Cleaning services
15. Handyman services
16. Interior decorating
17. Moving services
18. Personal training
19. Photography
20. Teaching a hobby

Figure 11 Side Hustles In Your Neighborhood

Side Hustles
In Your Community

1. Technology help
2. Personal coaching
3. Sports coaching
4. Child care
5. Senior care
6. Driving / ridesharing
7. Food delivery
8. Messenger services
9. Notary public
10. Renting out your car
11. Home rentals
12. Event catering
13. Event planning
14. Event emcee / DJ
15. Focus groups
16. Bookkeeping
17. Tax preparation
18. Cleaning services
19. Moving services
20. Flipping items

Figure 12 Side Hustles In Your Community

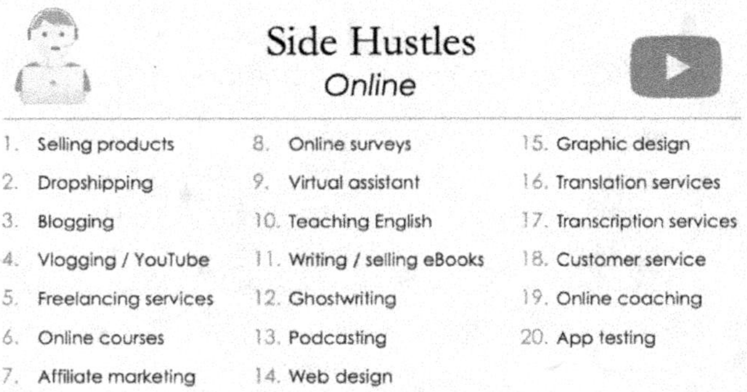

Side Hustles
Online

1. Selling products
2. Dropshipping
3. Blogging
4. Vlogging / YouTube
5. Freelancing services
6. Online courses
7. Affiliate marketing
8. Online surveys
9. Virtual assistant
10. Teaching English
11. Writing / selling eBooks
12. Ghostwriting
13. Podcasting
14. Web design
15. Graphic design
16. Translation services
17. Transcription services
18. Customer service
19. Online coaching
20. App testing

Figure 13 Side Hustles Online

CHAPTER NINE
References

1.   Kessler RC, Adler L, Barkley R, Biederman J, Conners CK, Demler O, Faraone SV, Greenhill LL, Howes MJ, Secnik K, Spencer T, Ustun TB, Walters EE, Zaslavsky AM. The prevalence and correlates of adult ADHD in the United States: results from the National Comorbidity Survey Replication. Am J Psychiatry. 2006 Apr;163(4):716-23. PMID: 16585449 [Based on diagnostic interview data from the National Comorbidity Survey Replication (NCS-R), the estimated prevalence of adults aged 18 to 44 years with a current diagnosis of ADHD is estimated. The overall prevalence of current adult ADHD is 4.4%.] Accessed November 14, 2019
https://www.nimh.nih.gov/health/statistics/attention-deficit-hyperactivity-disorder-adhd.shtml

2.   Verywell Mind. "ADHD Students May Have Poor Grades Due to Impaired Executive Functions." Accessed November 14, 2019.
https://www.verywellmind.com/what-are-executive-functions-20463.

3.   "Clarence Page Famous Living Confirmed Journalists

with ADHD." Accessed October 31, 2019. http://www.add-coach4u.com/famous-people-with-adhd/media/journalists/clarencepage.html.

4.   Putukian M , Kreher JB , Coppel DB , et al . Attention deficit hyperactivity disorder and the athlete: an American medical Society for sports medicine position statement. Clinical Journal of Sport Medicine 2011;21:392–400. CrossRefPubMedGoogle Scholar

5.   Daniel A. Lerner, Ingrid Verheul, Roy Thurik. Entrepreneurship and attention deficit/hyperactivity disorder: a large-scale study involving the clinical condition of ADHD. Accessed November 14, 2019
https://link.springer.com/article/10.1007/s11187-018-0061-1

6.   "The Mood-Boosting Power of Pets" Lawrence Robinson and Jeanne Segal, Ph.D. Accessed November 14, 2019
https://www.helpguide.org/articles/mental-health/mood-boosting-power-of-dogs.htm?pdf=13512

7.   "Nothing could stop me — not even ADD." "If I mess up, I mess up. I don't let ADD bring me down." Accessed November 14, 2019
https://www.addidutemag.com/famous-athletes-with-adhd/

8.   Allan Mamon Interview with MIC Accessed November 14, 2019

https://www.mic.com/articles/177801/how-two-teens-3-d-printed-a-fidget-spinner-empire-out-of-their-own-high-school

9.   "Teen With ADHD Builds a Fidget Empire." Accessed November 14, 2019.
https://www.understood.org/en/community-events/blogs/in-the-news/2017/07/24/teen-with-adhd-builds-a-fidget-empire.

About the Author

Connie Naresh is an entrepreneur, a teacher, a coach, a wife, and a mother.

She is raising her four energetic children with husband Yogi in Spokane, WA. Connie has formed a holistic body approach to managing ADHD and she is willing share her knowledge to help others seeking advice.

Connie's years of experience as a mother of ADHD children sent her on a continuous quest to find solutions to help her family to cope with ADHD both inside and outside the home. She is determined not to stop there. As a family coach, she encourages parents, young adults, and children in her community to implement strategies for directing ADHD strengths for one purpose: to achieve a positive outcome.

Connie is not writing from the position of a psychologist but from the viewpoint of a mother and a busy professional who manages the learning disabilities and focus challenges of her children and propose positive alternatives to often conventional thinking. Not only does she want to see her kids succeed, she also desires her readers to benefit from her experiences so they, too, can thrive under the most challenging of circumstances caused by ADHD.

When Connie set out to write her first book: Building a Successful Career with ADHD, she realized she has more to contribute than what would fit into one book dealing with ADHD. There are two additional books now in the works for a comprehensive series on Managing Life Successfully with ADHD for children and for adults.

If we were to sum up Connie's mission in one sentence, it would be this:

"Turning an ADHD weakness into a strength, a negative into a positive, and a challenge into an opportunity."

The Editor

How to Subscribe

To be the first to know about new book releases and resource updates, please subscribe to Connie's website advicewithconnie.com. A subscription will grant the reader direct access to a variety of resources and tools ready for download and print.

www.ingramcontent.com/pod-product-compliance
Lightning Source LLC
Chambersburg PA
CBHW050530280326
41933CB00011B/1534